GODDESSES OF INDIA

Ganga the Purifier of Sins

SHUBHA VILAS

Om KIDZ
An imprint of Om Books International

Goddess Ganga finds mention even in ancient Hindu texts like the Rigveda. Personified as a goddess, she has four arms and three eyes (to see the past, the present, and the future).

Ganga is well-ornamented with a crescent moon adorning her crown. She carries a lotus in one hand and a jar of jewels in another. The goddess rides a makara – half crocodile and half fish.

Once, the devatas were in a state of panic. The asura king Bali had defeated Indra and was creating havoc in the three lokas. To protect the devas, Vishnu appeared in his Vamanavatara and with three strides, one in each loka, banished the asuras.

Brahma then washed the feet of Vaman deva from the water in his kamandal, and Ganga was born from this holy water.

All was well for Ganga till something happened on Earth that changed her life. Sage Kapila burnt 60,000 sons of King Sagara, an ancestor of Sri Rama.

Sage Sagara's sons had thoughtlessly accused Sage Kapila of stealing their father's sacrificial horse that had, in fact, been stolen by Indra. Angered by their folly, Sage Kapila burnt all of them to ashes.

Sagara, horrified with his sons' death, asked the sage to purify their souls. Kapila revealed that the only way by which their souls could be purified was by washing their ashes with Ganga water. For that to happen, they needed the permission of Lord Brahma who held Ganga in his kamanadal.

Pleasing Brahma was not at all easy. King Sagara's last son Anshuman tried his best, but failed. Finally, it was the seventh generation of Sagara, King Bhagiratha, who put his heart and soul to succeed in pleasing Brahma.

At last, Brahma appeared but there was a problem. Ganga was wilful and powerful. If he released her, she would come down in a torrent and flood whatever came in her path. She had the strength to flood the entire Earth. So Brahma suggested that Bhagiratha pray to Lord Shiva to hold Ganga in his hair to reduce her force.

Bhagiratha prayed hard to Lord Shiva. Shiva agreed to help Bhagiratha. As soon as Brahma released her, Ganga, in her glory, descended on Earth at full speed. Shiva caught her in his hair. Not a single drop fell on Earth. After Ganga became calm, Shiva slowly released streams of her water on Earth as he had promised to Bhagiratha. He also told her to follow Bhagiratha and fulfil his mission.

Bhagiratha led Ganga to Sage Kapila's ashram. She still flowed with so much turbulence that it created a flood, destroying the hut and fields of Sage Jahnu on the way. The sage was so angered by Ganga's careless act that he swallowed her up fully to take revenge.

Brahma and Shiva were shocked. Bhagiratha was devastated. Feeling sorry for Bhagiratha, all the devatas prayed to Sage Jahnu and begged him to release Ganga. The sage calmed down soon and released Ganga from his ear. Since this was a rebirth for Ganga, she is also known as Jahnvi, daughter of Jahnu.

Finally they reached Sage Kapila's ashram where Ganga purified the 60,000 ancestors of Bhagiratha. Another name of Ganga is Bhagirathi, as she was invited by King Bhagiratha. The Ganga is said to have streams in the heavens, hell and on Earth.

Ever since then, simply touching her waters or chanting the name of Ganga is considered to grant salvation.

Since times immemorial till the present day, the Hindus have revered and worshipped the River Ganga as a goddess or Mother. People bathe in its holy waters to atone for their sins, ask to be forgiven and to purify themselves.